Heinemann InfoSearch

Raging Floods

Heinemann Library
Chicago, Illinois

Louise and Richard Spilsbury

Customer Service 888-454-2279
Visit our website at www.heinemannlibrary.com

Designed by David Poole and Paul Myerscough
Illustrations by Geoff Ward
Originated by Dot Gradations Limited
Printed in Hong Kong, China by Wing King Tong

07 06 05 04 03
10 9 8 7 6 5 4 3 2 1

Library of Congress Cataloging-in-Publication Data
Spilsbury, Louise.
  Raging floods / Louise and Richard Spilsbury.
      v. cm. -- (Awesome forces of nature)
Includes bibliographical references (p.   ).
Contents: What is a flood? -- What causes a flood? -- What are flash
floods? -- What happens in a flood? -- Who helps when floods happen? --
Case study: River Derwent, Yorkshire, UK -- Can floods be predicted? --
How do people prevent floods? -- Case study: coping with floods in
Bangladesh -- How about floods in the future?
  ISBN 1-4034-3724-6 (lib. bdg. : hardcover) -- ISBN 1-4034-4232-0 (pbk)

  1. Floods--Juvenile literature. [1. Floods.] I. Spilsbury, Richard,
1963- II. Title.
  GB1399.S65 2003
  363.34'93--dc21
                                                2003001109

Acknowledgments
The author and publisher are grateful to the following for permission to reproduce
copyright material:
Cover photograph by Associated Press.
pp. 4, 10, 12, 13, 16, 17, 18a, 19, 28 SIPA Press/Rex Features; p. 5 Karel Prinsloo/AP; p. 7 Arko
Datta/Reuters; p. 8 M. Barlow/Trip; p. 9 Grant McDowell/Nature Picture Library; p. 11
David Zalubowski/AP; p. 14 Panos Pictures; p. 15 J. Pat Carter/AP; pp. 18b, 22 David Hoffman/Still
Pictures; p. 20 Science Photo Library; p. 21 Andreas Buck/Das Fotoarchive; p. 23 Corbis; p. 24 H.
Rogers/Trip; p. 25 Nigel Dickenson/Still Pictures; p. 26 Powel Rahman; p. 27 AFP.

Some words are shown in bold, **like this.** You can find out what
they mean by looking in the glossary.

Contents

What Is a Flood?

A flood occurs when a normally dry area of land is covered by water. Floods are one of the most common natural disasters in the world. Floods can affect many different types of land, but they occur most often in places where flat, low-lying land meets rivers or seas. When sea or river levels rise, water spills out onto the land.

Important water

Water is necessary for living things. We drink water, wash in it, and cook with it. The plants and animals we eat also need water to survive. Yet, water can be very dangerous and damaging to people in a flood, especially if the flood comes without warning.

Water is heavy—just one bathful of water weighs about 1,600 pounds (750 kilograms). When water rushes quickly through streets or fields it becomes as powerful and damaging as a moving wall of concrete.

The power of floods

When water rushes through a town, it can damage buildings and bury houses under mud. It may drown people if they cannot get away in time. Even after the water finally drains away, there are still problems. In China in 1931, as many as 3.7 million people starved after a flood ruined their **crops.**

In Mozambique in 2001, many people had to wait a long time before being rescued. Water covered so many roads and bridges that rescue workers were unable to reach the flooded villages.

What Causes a Flood?

Water falls from the air onto land as rain or snow. Then, it drains into rivers and streams and eventually ends up in the ocean. Finally, the water **evaporates** from the ocean back into the air. This is called the water cycle. If a lot of water falls at once, it cannot all drain away immediately, so some stays on the surface of the land for a short time. This small amount of flooding is normal. Bad floods happen when very large amounts of water arrive on land in a short amount of time.

How does the water cycle work?

Most water that falls on land either drains into the soil as **groundwater,** collects in lakes and **reservoirs,** or forms ice at the **poles.** Living things use some of this stored water. The rest of the water that falls on land drains into rivers that flow into the oceans. Heat from the sun evaporates water from ocean surfaces. This means it turns liquid water into a gas or vapor in the air. When water vapor cools, it condenses—it changes back from vapor to liquid water. Droplets of the liquid water gather as clouds in the sky. The water then falls to Earth as rain, snow, or hail.

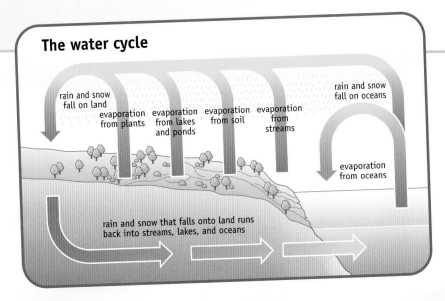

The water cycle

rain and snow fall on oceans

rain and snow fall on land

evaporation from plants

evaporation from lakes and ponds

evaporation from soil

evaporation from streams

evaporation from oceans

rain and snow that falls onto land runs back into streams, lakes, and oceans

When do floods happen?

In **temperate** parts of the world, such as the West Coast of the United States, flooding happens most often in spring and winter. These seasons are colder and wetter than summer and autumn. Large amounts of water fall during heavy spring rains, which sometimes last for days or weeks. Water also collects on land in spring when large amounts of snow or ice that built up over winter begin to melt.

In **tropical** countries, such as Kenya, it is warm all year. Most of the year's rainfall comes in one short, very wet season. This season is called the **monsoon.** There are often floods during monsoons. Floods can also come after sudden heavy rainstorms or when large waves of seawater caused by earthquakes, hurricanes, or typhoons hit land. Seawater floods can happen at any time on low-lying coastal land that is near **sea level.**

The monsoon season in India usually lasts from June to September. People in some parts of India expect floods during the monsoon.

Making matters worse

Some natural conditions make flooding more likely. If soil is frozen or waterlogged (full of **groundwater**), water that falls onto it cannot drain away. It then stays on top of the land and builds up, causing floods.

People also make things worse. They build **dams** and **reservoirs** to store water, but these occasionally break or overflow, releasing tons of water all at once. When people cut down trees to burn or to build with, wind blows away the top layer of soil that normally holds water. Without this **topsoil,** rainwater collects on the surface of the land. Also, in cities and towns, large areas of concrete around buildings and asphalt on roads stop water from soaking into the soil. Drains may not be big enough to take away the water quickly, so it stays on the surface.

In China, large areas of land have little or no topsoil because of flooding. Without topsoil, few plants can grow.

Can floods be a good thing?

Some areas flood regularly. Low-lying areas that are usually affected by river flooding are called **floodplains.** The floodplains and **deltas** of big rivers, such as the Nile in Egypt or the Mississippi in the United States, often flood during heavy rain.

In spite of the threat of floods, floodplains and deltas can be good places for people to live. After a flood, **nutrients** in the water soak into land, making it **fertile.** Some crops, such as rice, grow best in waterlogged soil.

What is a delta?

A river moves more slowly as it reaches an ocean. Bits of soil it is carrying drop to the river bottom forming a triangular area of land near the mouth of the river. This area is called a delta.

Land that will flood is cheap to buy and is fertile. This is why lots of people live on or near floodplains, despite the risks.

What Are Flash Floods?

Flash floods happen very suddenly—in a flash! Flash floods can happen with little or no warning and they can become extremely dangerous within a very short time.

Flash floods are usually caused by sudden heavy storms, where a huge amount of rain falls in a short time. When the rain collects in a stream or river, it turns these gentle waterways into raging torrents. Flash floods are particularly dangerous because people do not have time to get out of the way.

> "It's difficult to judge the depth, speed, and power of flood waters; in an instant, you can be swept into a drainage system or your car floated off a road or bridge." **Rocky Lopes, Disaster Services worker for the Red Cross**

Flash flood water moves very quickly, destroying buildings, pulling up trees, and rolling over cars in its path.

Fort Collins, Colorado, 1997

On the evening of July 28, 1997, the people of Fort Collins, Colorado, were sleeping peacefully. They were unaware of the disaster that was about to happen. It had been raining since midday and the water had been collecting behind a railway **embankment.** Suddenly, at 11 P.M., a wall of water two stories high crashed through the embankment. It smashed into two mobile home parks at the edge of the town.

"When we got there, there were children hanging on trees. We had people standing on mobile homes—people trapped. I've never seen anything like this in my life." Jim Pietrangelo, Fort Collins Fire Officer

CANADA

Fort Collins

Colorado **U.S.**

MEXICO

Five people drowned in the Fort Collins flash flood. Rescue workers saved over 100 people, though. The water destroyed homes and cars in its path.

What Happens in a Flood?

Floods change people's lives. They can affect a person's health, possessions, and work. Some effects of a flood can be dealt with quickly, but others last a long time.

Immediate health dangers

When a really bad flood suddenly hits a town, people can be swept away by rushing water or by walls of mud washed off the land. They may drown or be injured as they are washed away.

FLOOD ⚡ FACTS

! Since 1900, floods have killed more than 10,000 people in the United States alone.

! It only takes roughly 2 feet (60 cm) of water to float a car or even a bus.

! Most of the people killed by flash floods die because they try to outrun the water rather than climbing uphill out of its way.

This road bridge has been partly washed away by the force of a flood. The remaining part may have been weakened as well, so this man is putting himself in danger by standing so close to the edge.

Other hazards

Floating cars, trees, or rocks injure some people. Water can also knock down **power lines** and break gas and oil pipes. Electricity from the powerlines can **electrocute** anyone touching the water. If broken powerlines touch each other, they produce sparks. These sparks can cause fires in buildings. They can also cause explosions of gas and oil released from broken pipes.

Water, food, and shelter

Even though people are surrounded by flood water, they cannot drink it. The waste in people's drains, called **sewage,** mixes with drinking water in **reservoirs** and wells. This makes the tap water too **polluted** to drink.

People affected by flooding often have no food. Food supplies are washed away, polluted, or out of reach in buildings that are completely covered by water or mud. Farm animals may be washed away or drowned and farmers' **crops** may be ruined.

In a flood, people have little shelter. Their homes are sometimes washed away or full of water.

In 2002, a flood in southern Russia killed about 100 people and made about 100,000 homeless.

Long-term damage

After the rains stop and flood waters drain away, problems may continue. It takes a long time to clean and repair ruined houses, factories, and schools, and to clear streets. During that time, people may have to manage without homes, offices, and stores. Without **power lines** and telephone lines, people cannot operate machinery or get in touch with others. If roads, railways, bridges, and vehicles have been washed away or damaged, people cannot travel to work or leave to get food, water, or new clothes.

Polluted water, soggy materials, damp food, and dead animals are just the kinds of places that **viruses** and **bacteria** like to live. Viruses and bacteria cause dangerous diseases such as **dysentery,** which spreads when people drink polluted water. People with dysentery lose water through **diarrhea** and vomiting and become **dehydrated.** They need to drink clean water to get better, but after a flood, drinking water is often polluted—so it makes them even more sick.

When people clean up after floods, they often wear protective clothing. This keeps them safe from diseases or other hazards in the water.

What should people do in a flood?

If a flood happens, stay calm but act quickly to avoid dangers. You and your family should:

- keep a radio and/or mobile phone close by so you know what is happening;
- notify your neighbors, especially the elderly;
- be prepared to move to higher ground;
- try to avoid moving at night when you cannot see hazards;
- do what the emergency services (such as the police) tell you to do;
- keep out of flood water if possible, as it may be hazardous;
- if you have to get in the water, use a stick to test the depth of the water;
- keep away from power lines and from water near storm drains, as it moves fast;
- take pets with you when you move, or put them in a dry place with food. Three out of every ten pet owners risk their lives trying to rescue pets.

Never attempt to wade through floodwater. Wait somewhere safe until emergency service rescue workers come to rescue you.

Who Helps when Floods Happen?

Imagine you wake up one morning to find that your house is flooded with dirty water. Who will help?

The first people to arrive on the scene are workers from the emergency services. The police, fire department, and ambulance services make sure people are safe and treat any minor injuries. Local government and army workers help stop further flooding by making walls of sandbags. They also give out clean drinking water and food.

Emergency services may help people move to a safe place, away from the flood water and any hazards caused by flooding. This is called **evacuation.** Rescue workers may use boats, helicopters, and even divers to evacuate people.

Helpers use buildings such as gymnasiums as temporary shelters for flood victims. They bring in supplies of drinking water and food, dry clothes and blankets, and sometimes heaters.

Helping out

Poor people who live in poor countries may have to rely more on outside help when disaster strikes. Many local people may want to help but do not have the money to buy medicines and food. They do not usually have the equipment to help rescue people or give them shelter.

After bad floods, other countries and **charities** such as the Red Cross help by sending **aid.** Aid includes useful basic things such as dry food, plastic sheeting, and other materials to make shelters. It also includes pumps to remove water from buildings and medicines such as special drinks to prevent **dehydration.** Aid might also involve helping flood victims plan how to cope better with future floods.

Charities rely on people helping from a distance after a big flood. Donations (gifts) of money are used to provide aid for the victims.

Helping get back to normal

Once the flood waters have drained away, different help is needed to get life back to normal. This can take a very long time.

The first step is to see how much damage has been caused. Local governments hire engineers (machine experts) and builders to test the safety of damaged buildings, bridges, and roads. They decide whether they can be repaired or if they need to be rebuilt. Plumbers and electricians test and mend water pipes and **powerlines. Insurance** workers figure out how much it will cost to replace damaged things.

Possessions and household objects that were covered with **polluted** water usually need to be destroyed. This includes not only photos, books, and TVs, but also carpets, sofas, and cushions. When the house is empty it can be bleached all over to clean it. It then has to dry out. Each inch (2.5 cm) thickness of house brick takes more than two weeks to dry out.

It can take a long time for people to clean up. They have to shovel mud out of their homes or remove water with buckets or pumps.

River Derwent, Yorkshire, England, 1999

The River Derwent in Yorkshire, England, burst its banks in March 1999. More than 4.5 inches (12 cm) of rain had fallen in 48 hours and thick winter snow had melted from hills nearby. More than 100 homes in the towns of Old Malton and Norton were flooded, most up to their ground-floor ceilings. Some people moved upstairs in their houses to get above the flood. Others had to **evacuate** their houses because of hazards such as **sewage** in the flood water.

> "We didn't want to leave our house, despite the flood, but then it dawned on us—we were flushing the toilet right back into our own house."
> Di Keele, flood victim

After the water drained away, it took over six months for people's homes to dry out. The area flooded again in 2000, when another 170 homes were flooded.

NORTH YORKSHIRE

Scarborough
Old Malton
•Norton
York

The river was so swollen that many roads and bridges were under water or damaged. So, some residents could not get to banks or shops. They had to rely on food deliveries from boats.

Can Floods Be Predicted?

Floods destroy so much that people work very hard to predict when they might happen. They try to discover when and how bad weather will affect particular areas of land.

Weather

Forecasting, or predicting, weather accurately is not easy, but modern equipment helps. Scientists use **satellites** that are up in space to take pictures of clouds above Earth. The photos show how big the clouds are and how fast they are moving. The scientists use sensitive **radars** that can detect how much rain or snow is in the air. They also observe rainclouds and waves at sea from planes or helicopters.

People who work at weather stations collect even more information. They measure the amount of rain that falls each day, how fast snow and ice are melting, and how hot the air is. They record how fast the wind is blowing and how much water is in rivers, **reservoirs,** and lakes.

This photograph was taken by a satellite. It shows a spiral of clouds bringing wet weather to the land beneath.

Knowing the land

Bad weather will only cause a flood if the land cannot drain away the water quickly enough. Areas on tops of hills or with thick **topsoil** are less likely to flood than areas by a river or on hard rock. People record information such as how hilly the land is and how near it is to the sea or rivers. They store this information in computers and use it to make maps showing land that may flood in the future.

Flood risk

When heavy rains arrive, scientists look at how high rivers are and at weather forecasts to see how much more rain is expected. Then, using maps of the land and records of floods in the past, they warn people who are at risk from flooding.

If an area flooded in the past it will probably flood again in similar conditions. Many countries have recorded when and how high floods have been in years gone by. This man is showing the high water mark of a previous flood in the same location.

How Do People Prevent Floods?

In areas where floods can be predicted, people use different methods to try to prevent or reduce them. People control the amount of water in rivers by building **dams** and **flood barriers.** Large amounts of water that might cause flooding are then stored in **reservoirs.** People make the sides of rivers higher by building walls called **levees.** These walls help stop rivers from overflowing. People also dig drainage channels, so if rivers do overflow, the water drains away more easily. In coastal areas, people build sea walls to help keep waves off land.

Water runs faster off land where there is little **topsoil** to soak it up. In these places, people plant trees on hillsides around rivers and streams. The trees help stop topsoil **erosion**—when the soil is washed, blown, or rubbed away. Preventing erosion keeps the water from flowing more quickly toward **floodplains.**

The Thames flood barrier was built to prevent floods in London, England. It stops high sea **tides** from moving up the Thames River.

Building to control floods

In floodplains, floods often cannot be prevented, so people build villages, towns, and cities with the effects of flooding in mind. Houses are sometimes built on stilts so the owners can live above the flood waters. Houses are also built with materials that are not ruined by flood water. For example, they may have tiled concrete floors instead of wooden ones. **Power lines** and electrical sockets are positioned high on walls, and drainpipes can be blocked to keep **polluted** water from **sewage** pipes out of the house.

Sometimes houses are designed to keep water out. People may build watertight brick walls around houses or wells. They may also put special slots around doors and windows. When flood waters rise, they set floodboards—watertight doors—into the slots.

Acting like a sponge

Floodplains soak up large amounts of water like a sponge. The water then drains away slowly. When people build on floodplains, the land soaks up less water, so floods are more serious.

These houses have been built on stilts to protect them from flooding.

How do people prepare for floods?

Here are some things people need to do or have if a flood strikes:

- Flood kit—this kit might include a flashlight or lantern, a battery-powered or wind-up radio, a mobile phone, rubber gloves, rubber boots or waders, waterproof clothing, a first-aid kit, and blankets.

- **Insurance**—insurance helps pay to replace damaged or ruined possessions and buildings. Details of the insurance should be kept as part of the flood kit.

- Emergency list—this list includes useful phone numbers such as the emergency services and local flood information. People should know who is responsible for doing what during and after a flood.

- Safekeeping—store valuables and important documents, such as passports, upstairs or in a high and dry place.

The objects in a flood kit will only be useful if they can easily be found when a flood strikes. So, they should be packed together and stored safely.

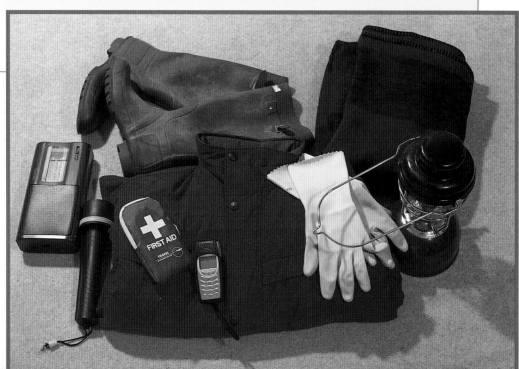

Can everyone prepare for floods?

The effects of flooding are hardest on poorer people. They cannot afford to build houses or roads that can survive floods. They cannot afford to buy insurance that would pay to rebuild their houses quickly if they are damaged by floods. They may live in countries that do not have the resources to predict floods accurately. They may not have radios, TVs, or telephones, which would alert them to a flood risk.

FLOOD FACTS

Governments in different countries have standard ways of telling their people how bad floods are.

! Flood Watch is the least serious. It means flooding is possible, so be aware of water levels and change travel plans.

! Severe Flood Warning is the most serious. It means severe flooding is expected. People should be prepared to lose power supplies and to do as the emergency services tell them if they have to **evacuate** their homes.

These houses in the Philippines have been severely damaged by flooding. Their owners may be too poor to rebuild the houses any stronger than they were before the flood.

Bangladesh

Bangladesh is a country in Asia where more than 100 million people live. It is at the **delta** of three major rivers—the Ganges, Brahmaputra, and Meghna. Each year during the **monsoon,** normal flooding affects a third of the country.

> "People in the rural areas know how to live with flooding, as they have learned from their **ancestors.** My straw and bamboo house would not be able to withstand the rush of flood water, so it can be taken apart and loaded onto my boat." Matbar Samad, from a village near Dhaka

Groups of villagers meet to discuss their flood plans before the monsoon season. They prepare by building walls around wells and **levees** along rivers. Families make and store medicines that treat the illnesses caused by flooding. They often keep ducks for fresh meat and eggs because ducks can swim. If they keep chickens—which cannot swim—they put them in cages that can float!

Bangladeshi children are taught how to use boats so they can use them during floods.

Disaster

Sometimes particularly bad floods happen in Bangladesh. In 1998, heavy monsoon rains and unusually high **tides** flooded more than two-thirds of the country for nine weeks. Thirty million people were affected. About 1,000 people were drowned, **electrocuted,** or bitten by poisonous snakes in the water.

Over the following months, many more people suffered as diseases such as **dysentery** spread. Food and drinking water became scarce.

Local flood planning could not cope. One flood shelter had only three toilets for 2,000 people. Ruined roads, bridges, and railroad tracks meant villages were cut off. Other countries and organizations helped by sending **aid,** including steel bridges and sacks of wheat. After the floods, the country built thousands of miles of new levees. But these levees may just push future floodwaters into different areas.

When roads and railway lines flood, many people cannot travel to work. It also means that deliveries of food or medicines may not reach people who need them.

What About Floods in the Future?

Scientists are noticing changes in the world's **climate.** Some of these changes are just the natural differences from year to year. Some are likely to be the result of global warming. This is when **pollution** in the atmosphere helps to increase the temperature on Earth. Global warming is causing ice at the **poles** to melt. This melting ice will cause a rise in **sea levels.** Global warming is also **evaporating** more water from the oceans, which may result in heavier storms that cause more floods.

Serious floods have always been part of life on Earth but they seem to be on the increase. We can all make an effort to learn how our activities affect climate and influence natural disasters such as flooding. Scientists are becoming better at predicting floods. We all must make sure that more people—rich and poor—are prepared when flood waters rise. With careful planning we can help make the floods of the future less damaging. Less damage means life can return to normal more quickly after disaster strikes.

Ten million people across the world are at constant risk of coastal flooding.

Major Floods of Recent Times

1970, Bangladesh
Heavy rains during a big typhoon caused floods that killed up to 500,000 people and left millions more homeless.

1991, Zhejiang province, China
Tai Hu, a lake at the mouth of the Yangtze River in China, flooded in 1991, covering an important industrial and agricultural region. More than 2,000 people died and a million homes were swept away. Overall, the flood affected the lives of 220 million people.

1993, Mississippi
More than 70,000 people were made homeless after floods in 1993 in Mississippi. Nearly 50,000 homes were damaged or destroyed and 52 people died. More than 11,000 square miles (30,000 square km) of farmland with crops and farm animals were ruined. Damage was estimated at between $15 and $20 billion—a huge amount of money.

1997, Poland and Germany
In 1997 the River Oder burst its banks, affecting over 1,000 cities, towns, and villages in Poland.

2000, Mozambique
After a **tropical** storm, two years' worth of rain fell in two weeks, leaving half a million people homeless. More than 700 people died and hundreds of thousands relied on food **aid.**

2002, Central Europe
In 2002 heavy August rainfall swelled the rivers Danube in Hungary, the Elbe in Germany, and the Vlatva in the Czech Republic to their highest levels in a century. Tens of thousands of people had to **evacuate** their homes in Prague, Budapest, and Dresden. Damage costs were around $20 billion.

Glossary

aid help given as money, medicine, food, or other essential items

ancestor relative in the past such as a great-great-grandparent

bacteria small living things that can cause diseases

charity group that collects money and gives out aid

climate usual weather patterns for an area

crop plant that is grown to eat

dam barrier built across a river to stop its normal flow. Dams are also used to store water in a reservoir.

dehydrated (dehydration) without enough water

delta triangular area of land where slow-moving river water meets the sea

diarrhea illness that causes watery bowel movements. Diarrhea can be very serious if not treated properly.

dysentery disease of the stomach caused by bacteria. Dysentery causes severe diarrhea and dehydration.

electrocute kill by electric shock

embankment raised road or railway

erosion wearing away by wind, water, or rubbing

evacuate (evacuation) remove people from a dangerous place until it is safe

evaporate (evaporating) when something turns from liquid to gas

fertile describes soil that produces lots of crops

flood barrier structure to control the flow of water in a river

floodplain area of land that normally floods after heavy rainfall

groundwater water found in soil or in cracks in rocks

insurance payments of small regular amounts of money to an insurance company to make sure repairs to damage after an accident or disaster such as a flood can be paid for

levee raised wall or bank at the edge of a river

monsoon wet season in parts of Asia, Africa, and elsewhere

nutrient chemical that is needed for growth and development

pole North Pole or South Pole—the most northerly and southerly places on Earth. They are covered in thick ice.

polluted (pollution) when something is spoiled and made unhealthy by something else

power line main cable that carries electricity

radar special machine that uses invisible rays to detect where things are

reservoir large natural or man-made lake used to store water

satellite object that goes around Earth in space. Satellites do jobs such as sending out TV signals or taking photographs.

sea level level of the sea surface
sewage waste matter from toilets and drains carried in sewers
temperate climate that is warm and dry in summer and wet and mild in winter
tide regular rise and fall of the sea
topsoil upper fertile layer of soil. Topsoil soaks up groundwater.
tropical from the Tropics, an area near the equator that is hot all year
virus tiny living things that can cause diseases

More Books to Read

Allen, Jean. *Floods*. Mankato, Minn.: Capstone Press, 2001.

Connolly, Sean. *Floods*. North Mankato, Minn.: Smart Apple Media, 2003.

Donnelly, Karen J. *Floods of the Past and Future*. New York: Rosen, 2003.

Egan, Lorraine Hopping. *Wild Weather: Floods!* Madison: Turtleback Books, 2000.

Richards, Julie. *Furious Floods*. Broomall, Penn.: Chelsea House, 2001. *An older reader can help you with this book.*

Sipiera, Diane M. and Paul P. *Floods*. Danbury, Conn.: Scholastic Library, 1999.

Index